LA LA LAND

FOR PIANO SOLO

MUSIC FROM THE MOTION PICTURE SOUNDTRACK

ISBN 978-1-5400-3590-5

HAL•LEONARD®

Visit Hal Leonard Online at
www.halleonard.com

World headquarters, contact:
Hal Leonard
7777 West Bluemound Road
Milwaukee, WI 53213
Email: info@halleonard.com

In Europe, contact:
Hal Leonard Europe Limited
1 Red Place
London, W1K 6PL
Email: info@halleonardeurope.com

In Australia, contact:
Hal Leonard Australia Pty. Ltd.
4 Lentara Court
Cheltenham, Victoria, 3192 Australia
Email: info@halleonard.com.au

ANOTHER DAY OF SUN

Music by JUSTIN HURWITZ
Lyrics by BENJ PASEK & JUSTIN PAUL

SOMEONE IN THE CROWD

Music by JUSTIN HURWITZ
Lyrics by BENJ PASEK & JUSTIN PAUL

Bright Broadway two-beat feel

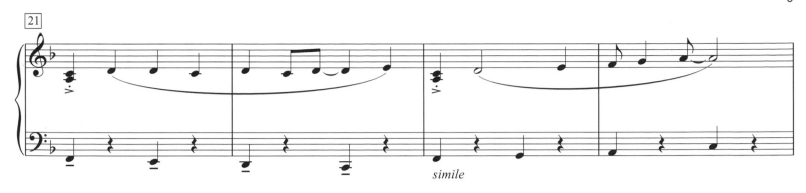

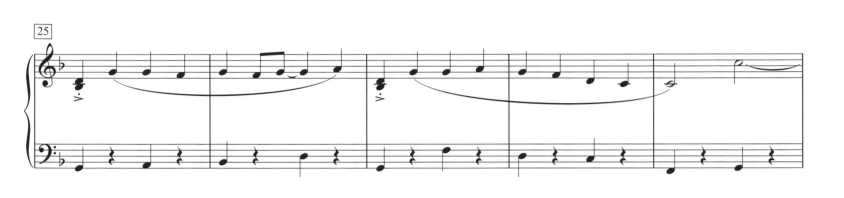

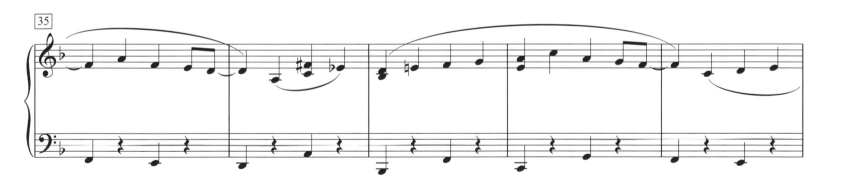

MIA & SEBASTIAN'S THEME

Music by
JUSTIN HURWITZ

CITY OF STARS

Music by JUSTIN HURWITZ
Lyrics by BENJ PASEK & JUSTIN PAUL

A LOVELY NIGHT

Music by JUSTIN HURWITZ
Lyrics by BENJ PASEK & JUSTIN PAUL

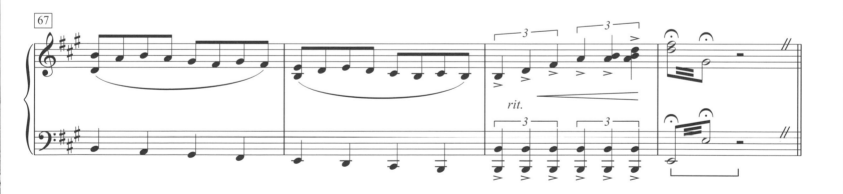

PLANETARIUM

Music by
JUSTIN HURWITZ

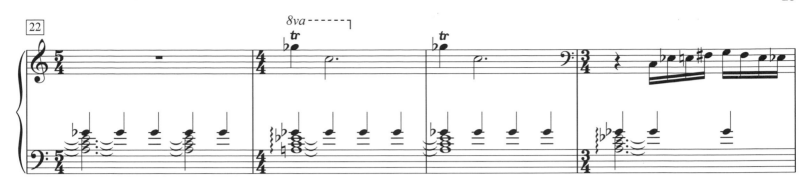

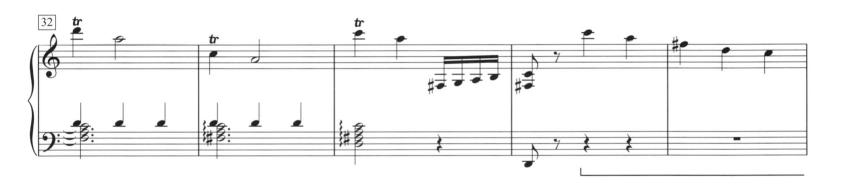

START A FIRE

Music & Lyrics by JOHN STEPHENS,
ANGÉLIQUE CINÉLU, MARIUS DE VRIES
and JUSTIN HURWITZ

ENGAGEMENT PARTY

Music by
JUSTIN HURWITZ

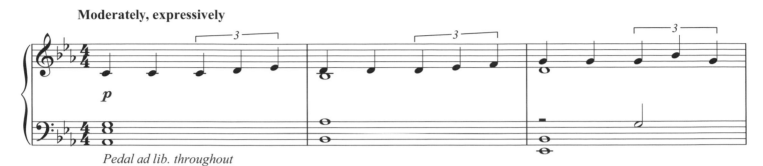

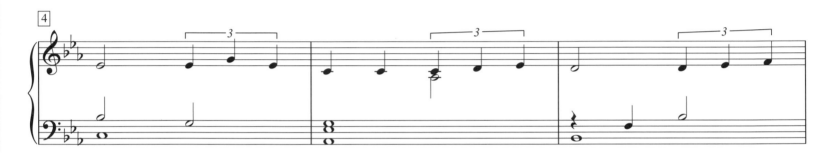

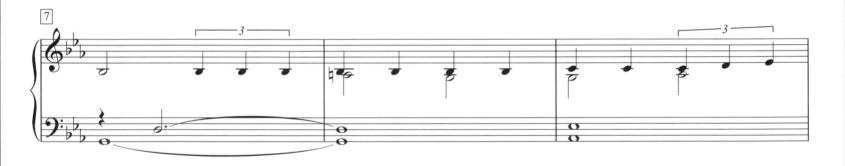

AUDITION
(The Fools Who Dream)

Music by JUSTIN HURWITZ
Lyrics by BENJ PASEK and JUSTIN PAUL

EPILOGUE

Music by
JUSTIN HURWITZ

Slowly, very freely

Pedal ad lib.

gradual accel.

Moderately, expressively

YOUR FAVORITE MUSIC
ARRANGED FOR PIANO SOLO

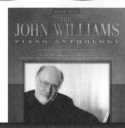

ARTIST, COMPOSER, TV & MOVIE SONGBOOKS

**Adele for Piano Solo –
3rd Edition**
00820186.............................$19.99

The Beatles Piano Solo
00294023.............................$17.99

**A Charlie Brown
Christmas**
00313176.............................$19.99

**Paul Cardall –
The Hymns Collection**
00295925.............................$24.99

Coldplay for Piano Solo
00307637.............................$17.99

**Selections from
Final Fantasy**
00148699.............................$19.99

**Alexis Ffrench - The
Sheet Music Collection**
00345258.............................$19.99

Game of Thrones
00199166.............................$19.99

Hamilton
00354612.............................$19.99

**Hillsong Worship
Favorites**
00303164.............................$14.99

How to Train Your Dragon
00138210.............................$22.99

Elton John Collection
00306040.............................$24.99

La La Land
00283691.............................$16.99

John Legend Collection
00233195.............................$17.99

Les Misérables
00290271.............................$22.99

Little Women
00338470.............................$19.99

Outlander: The Series
00254460.............................$19.99

**The Peanuts®
Illustrated Songbook**
00313178.............................$29.99

**Astor Piazzolla –
Piano Collection**
00285510.............................$19.99

**Pirates of the Caribbean –
Curse of the Black Pearl**
00313256.............................$22.99

Pride & Prejudice
00123854.............................$17.99

Queen
00289784.............................$19.99

John Williams Anthology
00194555.............................$24.99

George Winston Piano Solos
00306822.............................$2?.99

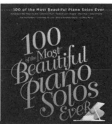

MIXED COLLECTIONS

**Beautiful Piano
Instrumentals**
00149926.............................$19.99

**Best Jazz
Piano Solos Ever**
00312079.............................$27.99

**Big Book of
Classical Music**
00310508.............................$24.99

Big Book of Ragtime Piano
00311749.............................$22.99

Christmas Medleys
00350572.............................$16.99

Disney Medleys
00242588.............................$19.99

Disney Piano Solos
00313128.............................$17.99

Favorite Pop Piano Solos
00312523.............................$17.99

Great Piano Solos
00311273.............................$19.99

**The Greatest Video
Game Music**
00201767.............................$19.99

Most Relaxing Songs
00233879.............................$19.99

**Movie Themes
Budget Book**
00289137.............................$14.99

**100 of the Most Beautiful
Piano Solos Ever**
00102787.............................$29.99

100 Movie Songs
00102804.............................$32.99

Peaceful Piano Solos
00286009.............................$19.99

**Piano Solos for
All Occasions**
00310964.............................$24.99

Sunday Solos for Piano
00311272.............................$17.99

Top Hits for Piano Solo
00294635.............................$16.99

HAL•LEONARD®
View songlists online and order from your
favorite music retailer at
halleonard.com